Little Hymns • *Jesus Loves The Little Children*
Written and illustrated by Andy Holmes
Watercolor by Cameron Thorp
Music transcription by Marty Franks

Copyright ©1993 by HSH Educational Media Company
P.O. Box 167187, Irving, Texas 75016

First Printing 1993
ISBN 0-929216-56-3
Printed in the United States of America

Published by

PRESS

Little Hymns®

by Andy Holmes

Jesus Loves The Little Children

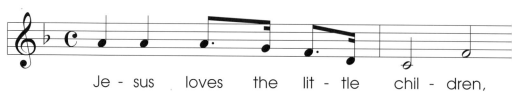

Je - sus   loves   the   lit - tle   chil - dren,

All   the   chil - dren   of   the   world.

Red and yel - low, black and white,

They are pre - cious in His sight;

Je - sus   loves the lit - tle chil - dren of the   world.

Je - sus   blessed   the   lit - tle   chil - dren,

All the chil - dren of the world;

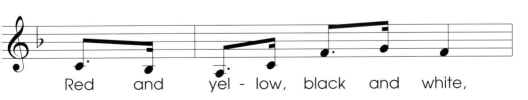

Red and yel - low, black and white,

They are pre - cious in His sight;

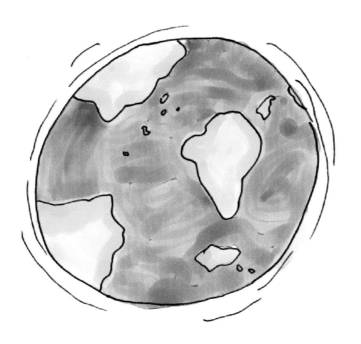

Je - sus blessed the lit - tle chil - dren of the world.

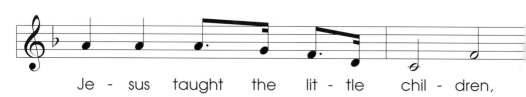

Je - sus taught the lit - tle chil - dren,

All the chil - dren of the world;

Red and yel - low, black and white,

They are   pre - cious   in   His   sight;

Je - sus taught the lit - tle chil - dren of the world.

Je - sus died for all the chil - dren,

All   the   chil - dren   of   the   world;

Red and yel - low, black and white,

They are pre - cious in His sight;

Je - sus   died   for   all   the chil - dren   of   the   world.

Jesus Loves The Little Children

Je - sus loves the lit - tle chil - dren, All the chil - dren of the
Je - sus blessed the lit - tle chil - dren, All the chil - dren of the
Je - sus taught the lit - tle chil - dren, All the chil - dren of the
Je - sus died for all the chil - dren, All the chil - dren of the

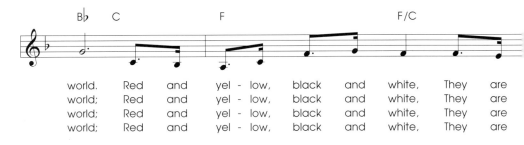

world. Red and yel - low, black and white, They are
world; Red and yel - low, black and white, They are
world; Red and yel - low, black and white, They are
world; Red and yel - low, black and white, They are

pre - cious in His sight; Je - sus loves the lit - tle chil - dren of the world.
pre - cious in His sight; Je - sus blessed the lit - tle chil - dren of the world.
pre - cious in His sight; Je - sus taught the lit - tle chil - dren of the world.
pre - cious in His sight; Je - sus died for all the chil - dren of the world.